W9-ATY-452

Seven Natural Wonders of ASIA *and the* MIDDLE EAST

Michael Woods and Mary B. Woods

TWENTY-FIRST CENTURY BOOKS
Minneapolis

To the Fairfax County Public Schools' librarians

Twenty-First Century Books
A division of Lerner Publishing Group, Inc.
241 First Avenue North
Minneapolis, MN 55401 U.S.A.

Website address: www.lernerbooks.com

Library of Congress Cataloging-in-Publication Data

Woods, Michael, 1946–
Seven natural wonders of Asia and the Middle East / by Michael Woods and Mary B. Woods.
p. cm. – (Seven wonders)
Includes bibliographical references and index.
ISBN 978–0–8225–9073–6 (lib. bdg. : alk. paper)
1. Landforms—Asia—Juvenile literature. 2. Landforms—Middle East—Juvenile literature. 3. Landscape—Asia—Juvenile literature. 4. Landscape—Middle East—Juvenile literature. I. Woods, Mary B. (Mary Boyle), 1946– II. Title.
GB437.W66 2009
508.5–dc22 2008027605

Manufactured in the United States of America
1 2 3 4 5 6 – DP – 14 13 12 11 10 09

Contents

Introduction

People love to make lists of the biggest and the best. Almost twenty-five hundred years ago, a Greek writer named Herodotus made a list of the most awesome things ever built by people. The list included buildings, statues, and other objects that were large, wondrous, and impressive. Later, other writers added new items to the list. Writers eventually agreed on a final list. It was called the Seven Wonders of the Ancient World.

The list became so famous that people began imitating it. They made other lists of wonders. They listed Seven Wonders of the Modern World and Seven Wonders of the Middle Ages. People even made lists of undersea wonders.

People also made lists of natural wonders. Natural wonders are extraordinary things created by nature, without help from people. Earth is full of natural wonders, so it has been hard for people to choose the absolute best. Over the years, different people have made different lists of the Seven Wonders of the Natural World.

This book explores seven natural wonders from Asia and the Middle East. Like Earth as a whole, Asia and the Middle East have far more than seven natural wonders. But even if people can never agree on which ones are the greatest, these seven choices are sure to amaze you.

Wonderful Places

Asia is the largest continent on Earth. It stretches from the Arctic Ocean in the north to the Indian Ocean in the south. It borders the Pacific Ocean in the east and Europe in the west. Fifty countries are part of Asia. They include India, Nepal, China, Vietnam, the Philippines, Indonesia, and Japan. More than 60 percent of the world's people live in Asia. The total population of Asia is about 3.8 billion.

The Middle East includes lands around the eastern and southern shores of the Mediterranean Sea, as well as lands around the Persian Gulf. More than a dozen modern countries occupy that region. They include Egypt, Iran, Iraq, Saudi Arabia, Lebanon, Syria, Israel, and Jordan.

Asia and the Middle East contain hundreds of different landscapes. Deserts cover much of Saudi Arabia. Rain forests grow in Indonesia. Nepal is home to rugged mountains. Northern Asia is cold and icy. The south is hot and humid. The region's animals are just as diverse. They range from the camels in the western and central deserts to orangutans in the southeast to reindeer in the north. Millions of different plants make their homes in Asia as well.

Wonderful Adventure

This book will visit some of the most amazing natural wonders of Asia and the Middle East. The first stop will be at Mount Everest, the world's highest mountain, part of the vast Himalaya mountain chain. We'll also stop at the bleak Gobi Desert in central Asia. Travelers to this rugged desert have reported mysterious sights and sounds. We'll visit the Sumatra rain forest, where orangutans, tigers, and other fascinating animals make their homes. In the salty waters of the Dead Sea, between Israel and Jordan, we will swim but never sink. Other awe-inspiring wonders are waiting in between those visits. Turn the page to begin your adventure.

The blue-webbed gliding frog is one of the many rare animals that live in the Sumatra rain forest.

1 Mount Everest

Snow and ice cover the north face of Mount Everest. High winds sometimes blow snow cover away, exposing rock faces and gravel slopes on the mountainside.

SOME LOCAL PEOPLE CALL THE MOUNTAIN CHOMOLUNGMA, OR "MOTHER GODDESS OF THE WORLD." OTHERS CALL IT SAGARMATHA, OR "GODDESS OF THE SKY." IN THE 1800S, MAPMAKERS CALLED IT SIMPLY PEAK 15. IN MODERN TIMES, MOST PEOPLE CALL IT MOUNT EVEREST. BY ANY NAME, IT IS THE TALLEST MOUNTAIN IN THE WORLD.

Mount Everest is 29,035 feet (8,850 meters) tall. That means it towers 5.5 miles (8.9 kilometers) above Earth's surface. Many airplanes can't even fly that high.

Mount Everest is one of more than one hundred peaks in the Himalayas, or Himalaya mountains. This big chain of mountains runs along the border between China and India. The Himalayas form an arc, or curve, that stretches for 1,500 miles (2,414 km).

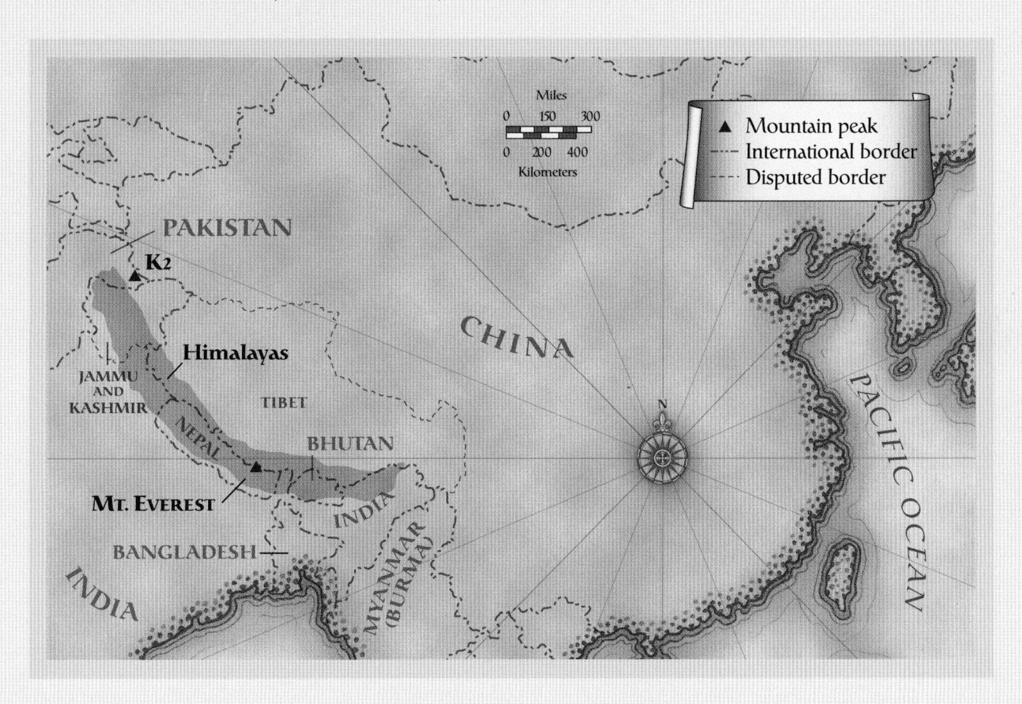

On its northern end, the chain begins in the territory of Jammu and Kashmir (claimed by both India and Pakistan). It then stretches southeast through northern India, Tibet, the nations of Nepal and Bhutan, and again into India. Mount Everest sits between Nepal and Tibet.

Land of Snow

If you've ever visited mountains, you know that the weather gets colder the higher you go. It's not uncommon to see snow on the top of tall mountains, even in summer.

The Himalayas are taller than any other mountains. Their tops are always covered in snow, summer and winter. In fact, the name *Himalaya* comes from an ancient word meaning "land of snow." In July, the warmest month, the air on top of Mount Everest is still bitter cold. The average July temperature

K2

The world's second-highest mountain is also in the Himalayas. It is K2, or Mount Godwin Austen. Located in the territory of Jammu and Kashmir, the mountain is 28,250 feet (8,611 m) high. It is part of the Karakoram Range in the northwestern Himalayas. Henry Haversham Godwin-Austen, a British surveyor, mapped the mountain in 1856. The *K* in the name stands for "Karakoram." The number 2 means it was the second peak that Godwin-Austen observed as he approached the mountains.

When scientists measure the height of a mountain, they subtract the height added by snow and ice. Climbers have measured up to 10 feet (3 m) of snow and ice on Everest's peak.

Above: ***Smaller peaks surround Mount Everest (center).***
Inset: ***A mountaineer climbs Mount Everest in a blizzard. Blizzards can blind climbers or push them off balance.***

is –2°F (–19°C). In January, the coldest month, temperatures average –33°F (–36°C). On really cold days, temperatures can dip to –76°F (–60°C). At this temperature, bare skin will freeze in seconds.

Fierce snowstorms often sweep over Mount Everest. Winds howling at more than 100 miles (160 km) per hour can whip the snow into blizzards. During these storms, it is often impossible to see through the snow. Blizzards may last for days at a time. The strong blizzard winds make Everest's cold temperatures feel even colder.

Two Sherpas take a break as their yaks rest and graze. Sherpas sometimes ride yaks, but the animals usually carry heavy loads while the people guide them on foot.

Sacred Mountains

Mount Everest is far too high and far too cold for humans to live there. But people called Sherpas have lived in villages beneath the mountain for centuries.

Traditionally, Sherpas made a living by growing crops and raising yaks. Yaks are long-haired animals, related to cows. Sherpas used yak wool to make clothing and other textiles. They drank yak milk and ate yak meat. Sherpas also used yaks like trucks. The animals carried the Sherpas' heavy loads over rough mountain paths.

Sherpas believe that the Himalaya mountains are sacred. In past centuries, Sherpas never climbed the mountains. They thought that evil spirits lived on the high peaks.

Mapping the Mountains

In the 1700s, Great Britain began to rule India. The British sent mapmakers to study the land. In the mid-1800s, George Everest, a British geographer and engineer, mapped a large section of India, including the Himalayas.

George Everest spent twenty-five years studying the Himalayas. In 1861 the British government honored him for his contributions to science.

Ever *Wonder?*

How did Andrew Scott Waugh measure Mount Everest in 1852? He used trigonometry. This branch of mathematics involves the relationship between the sides and angles of triangles. It helped Waugh and his team measure Mount Everest from almost 160 miles (257 km) away. The measurements were amazingly accurate. The British mapmakers figured that Mount Everest was 29,002 feet (8,839 m) high—only 33 feet (10 m) less than its actual height. In modern times, people use high-tech devices to measure mountains. For instance, they use electronic sensors on satellites out in space.

The British mapmakers had a simple system for naming the mountains of the Himalayas. They called the first peak that came into view Peak 1. The fifteenth mountain they saw was Peak 15.

It is hard to tell from the ground which mountain in the Himalayas is the tallest. Using mathematics, surveyor Andrew Scott Waugh measured Peak 15 in 1852. Waugh determined that the mountain was more than 29,000 feet (8,840 m) high. That meant it was the tallest mountain in the world. Waugh named this monster mountain Mount Everest, after George Everest.

This satellite image shows Mount Everest (center) *surrounded by the peaks and valleys of the Himalayas.*

Climb Every Mountain

After Andrew Waugh showed that Everest was the world's highest mountain, people dreamed of climbing to the top. This would be a difficult task, however. The higher you go above Earth's surface, the thinner the air becomes. That is, the air contains less oxygen. At high altitudes, people who don't normally live in the mountains have difficulty breathing. They huff and puff. They get exhausted easily. Some become very ill.

Sherpas, however, are used to thin air. They normally make their homes at about 14,000 feet (4,267 m) above sea level. European mountain climbers realized that Sherpas could help them climb Mount Everest. The climbers hired Sherpas to carry their food and equipment.

For almost one hundred years, teams of climbers tried to reach Mount Everest's peak. Every team turned back before reaching the top, however. Cold weather, fierce winds, exhaustion, and sickness forced them to give up. Many climbers died.

In 1953 New Zealand mountain climber Edmund Hillary and Nepalese Sherpa Tenzing Norgay reached the peak of Mount Everest. They became almost as famous as the first astronauts who later walked on the moon.

After Hillary and Norgay, more climbers scaled Mount Everest. By 2008 almost 2,200 people had reached the top. Climbing the mountain can take weeks. It requires special clothing and equipment.

Two Sherpa porters carry supplies past a Buddhist monument on a Mount Everest trail.

Did You *Know?*

In May 2008, in honor of the upcoming Olympics in Beijing, China, climbers carried the Olympic torch to the top of Mount Everest.

"We looked around in wonder. We had reached the top of the world."

—Edmund Hillary, 1953

Above: *On clear days, the view from the summit of Mount Everest extends across the Himalayas.* Below: *Edmund Hillary* (left) *and Tenzing Norgay* (right) *rest in camp after returning from the mountain's summit.*

THE WORLD'S TALLEST *Graveyard*

About one out of every ten people who try to climb Mount Everest dies in the attempt. Since 1852 more than two hundred people have died on the mountain. On a single day in 1996, eight climbers froze to death in a storm.

Climbers usually travel in groups. They hire guides and Sherpas to help them. Some climbers pay more than forty thousand dollars for guides to lead them up the mountain.

Making Mountains

The tall Himalaya mountains are getting even taller! To understand why, we need to know how mountains form in the first place. The process begins with Earth's crust, or outer layer. The crust consists of about thirty tectonic plates. The plates are gigantic slabs of rock. They move about 1 to 2 inches (3 to 6 centimeters) each year. Sometimes, two plates grind together with enormous force. When this happens, one plate slips below the other. The top plate moves upward. Over thousands of years, this upward movement creates mountains. About 30 million years ago, the Indian-Australian Plate and the Eurasian Plate began pushing against each other. Over time, this pushing created the Himalayas.

Both plates continue to grind against each other. As a result, the Himalayas are getting higher. They grow by about 2.4 inches (6.1 cm) per year. That growth may sound small. However, if it continues for twenty-six thousand years, the Himalayas will stand almost 5,000 feet (1,524 m) higher than they do in our era.

Monster Mountains' *Monster?*

According to an ancient legend, a monster lives in the Himalaya mountains. People call the monster the Yeti or the Abominable Snowman *(below)*. The snowman is said to be a tall apelike creature. It walks on two legs. Its body is covered with long, dark hair. Some climbers on Mount Everest have reported seeing such a creature. Others have reported seeing monstrous footprints in the snow. Skeptics, or disbelievers, say there is no such thing as a Yeti. They say the giant footprints were probably made by bears.

> *"Because it is there."*
>
> —*British explorer George Mallory, explaining why people try to climb Mount Everest, 1923*

Worries about the Wonder

Almost one million people visit the Mount Everest area each year. Only a small number of those visitors try to climb the mountain. The rest enjoy the view from below. The visitors help the local economy. They spend their money in hotels and restaurants. They buy homemade crafts as souvenirs.

However, the tourists also hurt the environment. Climbers on Mount Everest have no place to dispose of empty bottles, food wrappers, and other trash. Carrying trash back down the mountain is difficult. So climbers often leave it behind. The trash has piled up. Some people have even called Mount Everest the world's highest junkyard.

The Nepalese government and private organizations are working to remove the trash from Everest. Teams have climbed the mountain just to clean up the junk. Nepal is trying to protect Mount Everest in other ways. In 1976 Nepal established Sagarmatha National Park. This park includes parts of Mount Everest. China, on the other side of the mountain, has established thirteen nature preserves near Mount Everest. These preserves cover about 126,000 square miles (326,000 sq. km).

In 1979 the United Nations Educational, Scientific, and Cultural Organization (UNESCO) declared Sagarmatha National Park to be a World Heritage Site. World Heritage Sites are places of great importance to all of humanity. UNESCO tries to protect and preserve these sites for future generations.

In 2001 mountaineers Ken Noguchi (left) *and Sang Bae Lee* (right) *mounted an expedition to remove garbage from Mount Everest. They collected more than 3,500 pounds (1,600 kilograms) of trash left by mountain climbers.*

2 The Gobi Desert

The Khongoryn Els sand dunes of Mongolia are part of the Gobi Desert. Strong winds blow the sand into hills that can reach more than 2,600 feet (792 m) in height.

In 1295 Italian explorer Marco Polo returned to Venice, Italy, with amazing stories about his travels. For twenty-four years, Polo had traveled around China and central Asia. Niccolo Polo and Maffeo Polo—Marco's father and uncle—had traveled with him. They were the first Europeans to see and describe many parts of Asia.

One of Marco's stories was spooky. He told about crossing a vast desert in about 1275. The trip through this dry land took weeks. Polo said that the desert was haunted. He described how expedition members sometimes heard mysterious voices calling to them in the desert. They also heard weird booms, whirls, and whooshes. They sometimes saw people in the distance. When they tried to approach, the people vanished into thin air.

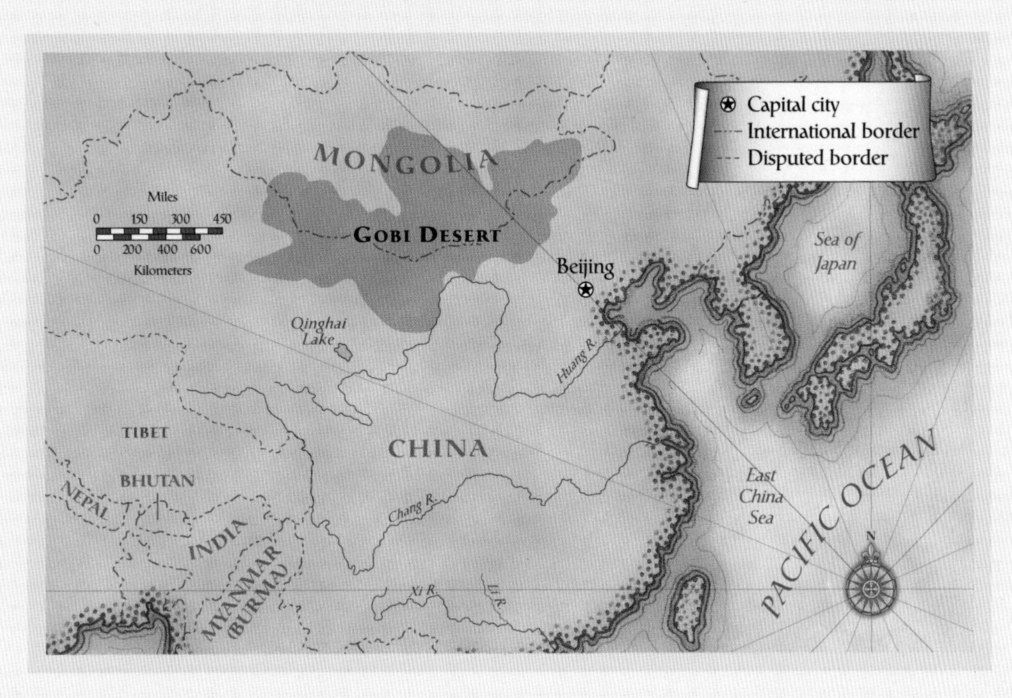

"When a man is riding through this desert by night and for some reason . . . gets separated from his companions . . . he hears spirit voices talking to him as if they were his companions, sometimes even calling him by name. Often these voices lure him away from the path and he never finds it again."

—Marco Polo, Description of the World, 1298

Marco Polo was talking about the Gobi Desert in northern China and southern Mongolia. The Gobi is the largest desert in Asia. It covers an area about 1,000 miles (1,600 km) long and 600 miles (965 km) wide.

Hot and Cold

Deserts are dry regions. Most scientists define deserts as places that receive less than 10 inches (25 cm) of precipitation (rain and snow) per year. Deserts cover about one-fifth of the land on Earth.

Some deserts, such as the Sahara in northern Africa, are scorchingly hot. But not all deserts are hot. Some deserts are cold places, covered by ice and snow. In fact, the world's biggest desert is the continent of Antarctica. There, temperatures can drop to −100°F (−73°C).

Although the Gobi Desert isn't as cold as Antarctica, it is still a cold desert. It has long, cold winters and short, hot summers. Winter temperatures average around 10°F (−12°C), but sometimes winter temperatures drop to −40°F (−40°C). In summer, temperatures average about 70°F (21°C).

Patches of snow cling to the ground in the Gobi desert region of southwestern Mongolia.

Small plants grow along the edges of canyons in the Gobi in southern Mongolia. Desert plants grow quickly during infrequent periods of rainfall. They produce seeds that can survive long periods without water.

The southeastern part of the Gobi is bone dry. It gets almost no rain. The rest of the Gobi gets 8 to 10 inches (20 to 25 cm) of rain and snow each year.

Desert Magic

A Mongolian legend says that a powerful ruler used magic to create the Gobi Desert. According to the story, an invading army forced the ruler to leave his kingdom. While fleeing, he cast a spell on the land. The spell made the land dry up. It became a desert, without food or water for the invaders.

Scientists explain the Gobi Desert differently. Their explanation involves the Himalaya mountains, southwest of the desert. When wet air passes over the Himalayas, it rises high into the atmosphere. The air cools as it rises. Then it releases its moisture, in the form of snow, on the mountains. By the time the air reaches the other side of the Himalayas, it is dry. In this way, the mountains act like a wall that prevents rain and snow from reaching the Gobi.

"In this desert there are a great many evil demons. There also are . . . winds which kill all who encounter them. There are no birds or beasts to be seen, but so far as the eye can reach, the route is marked by the blackened bones of men who have perished in an attempt to cross the desert."

—Chinese traveler and religious scholar Fahsien, circa A.D. 400

Flat plains covered in gravel make up much of the Gobi. This section of the desert lies in China, near a highway that follows trading routes established by Marco Polo and his fellow merchants.

A sudden sandstorm in the Gobi desert looms in front of a jeep on the Mongolian plain.

Ever *Wonder?*

What happens to the billions of tons of soil swept into the air during Gobi Desert sandstorms? Some of it may land on you. Winds high in Earth's atmosphere carry Gobi Desert dust around the world. Scientists have found dust from the Gobi Desert in California and other parts of the western United States. Scientists worry that the dust may be harmful to people. Some of the dust contains dangerous chemicals used in farming. Other dust carries germs that can make people sick.

Sights, Sounds—and Sand

Gobi is a word in the Mongolian language. It means "gravel-covered plain." That name accurately describes the Gobi Desert. Much of the desert is a flat plain. Small stones, gritty soil, and dust cover the land. In some areas, the wind has piled up sand into huge, rippled sand dunes. Winds whipping across these dunes can produce the weird sounds that Marco Polo described in his writings.

The hot desert air also produces mirages, or optical illusions. In other words, people traveling in the desert sometimes see things that don't really exist. Perhaps that explains the strange sights that Marco Polo mentioned.

The Gobi Desert is very windy. Strong winds often roar at speeds of almost 90 miles (145 km) per hour. The wind whips sand and dirt into the air. The blowing sand stings people's skin. People and animals can't walk through the fierce storms. It's impossible to see through the sand. Even cars and trucks can't travel during sandstorms.

Homes in the Desert

Harsh temperatures, low rainfall, and strong winds make the Gobi Desert a difficult place to live. But the desert also has oases, or areas with underground springs and wells. In addition, lands around the edges of the desert are wetter than those in the center. In the wet areas, grasses and bushes grow. The water and plants help people and animals to live in the desert.

Some people travel through the desert with herds of goats, sheep, and cattle. They move from place to place, looking for water and fresh grass for their animals. Wild animals also live in the desert. These animals include antelopes, foxes, rabbits, wolves, and birds. One of the most interesting animals is the Gobi bear. It is the only bear in the world that lives in a desert.

A Mongolian woman milks her goats in her camp in the Gobi. Her home is a round tent called a yurt. Traditional yurts have walls made of strips of lightweight wood and a roof held up by poles. These supports are covered with thick pieces of felt, which keep out wind, snow, and sand. When herders need to move on to fresh grazing land, they pack up the yurt and pull it to the next camp using a pack horse.

Bactrian camels graze at the edge of the Gobi. Not only can camels survive for long periods without water, but they can also withstand extreme temperatures. These traits help them to live in the Gobi, where very cold nights can follow hot days.

Historic *Gobi*

People have lived in and traveled through the Gobi Desert for centuries. In ancient times, the Silk Road passed through the Gobi Desert. The road was a group of trade routes between Asia and the Middle East. Merchants *(below)* traveled the routes with shipments of silk, spices, and other trade goods. They used camels to carry their heavy loads. In the 1200s and 1300s, people called the Mongols ruled a vast empire in central Asia. Mongol armies often traveled through the Gobi Desert.

Another interesting desert dweller is the wild Bactrian camel. Bactrian camels have two humps. Unlike domesticated (tame) Bactrian camels, wild Bactrian camels do not live among people. Fewer than one thousand wild Bactrian camels are left on Earth. Some of them live in the Gobi Desert. Others live in different parts of China.

Worries about the Wonder

The biggest worry about the Gobi Desert is that it is getting bigger. More and more families are herding goats and other animals on grasslands along the desert's edges. Big herds of animals eat a lot of grass. They eat it faster than new grass can grow.

Above: *The Great Wall of China follows the southern border of the Gobi. This section of the wall lies on the desert's southwestern side.* Below: *Shallow ditches direct water to fields of winter wheat at the edge of the Gobi in central China.*

DINOSAUR *Desert*

In 1923 U.S. scientist Roy Chapman Andrews led an expedition to the Gobi Desert to search for dinosaur bones. He thought that dinosaurs probably lived in the area millions of years ago, when the weather was wetter. Andrews discovered the bones of a previously unknown dinosaur. Compared to other dinosaurs, it was small. It was about 6 feet (1.8 m) long.

Andrews named the dinosaur *Oviraptor*. This name comes from Latin words meaning "egg thief." Andrews thought the *Oviraptor* ate other dinosaurs' eggs. Later, scientists determined that the *Oviraptor* probably ate different kinds of food, such as small animals.

In 1993 scientists found a skeleton of an *Oviraptor* sitting on a nest of fossilized eggs *(below)*. The dinosaur looked a lot like a modern bird in a nest. This discovery helped show that modern birds are probably descended from dinosaurs.

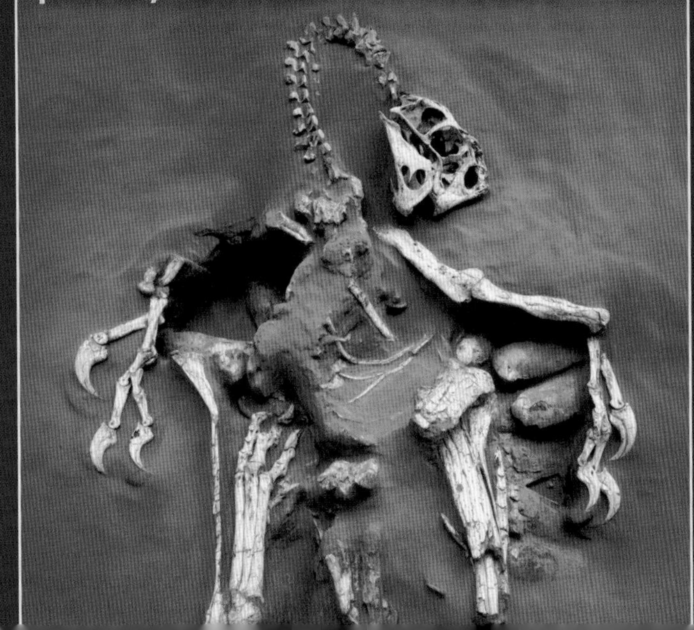

Once the grass is gone, the bare soil absorbs more heat from the sun. The land gets drier. In addition, overgrazing kills plant roots, which normally hold the soil in place.

People on the edges of the Gobi are also plowing grasslands to grow barley, wheat, grapes, and other crops. Plowing also destroys plant roots. Without roots to act as an anchor, soil blows away in the wind.

Because of overgrazing and plowing, grasslands on the edges of the Gobi are turning to desert. This process is called desertification. Each year, the Gobi Desert expands by an area equal to the size of one million high school football fields.

The Chinese government is trying to stop the Gobi's growth. The government encourages herders to graze fewer animals. Some groups plant hardy grasses and shrubs on the edges of the desert. These plants will help hold the soil in place. Even though the Gobi Desert is a wondrous place, people do not want this wonder to grow any bigger.

3 Mount Fuji

The still waters of Lake Yamanaka reflect Mount Fuji's snow-covered peak. Mount Fuji can be seen from Japan's capital city, Tokyo. Many of the city's residents enjoy weekend trips to the mountain.

MOUNT FUJI IS A BEAUTIFUL CONE-SHAPED MOUNTAIN IN JAPAN. AT 12,388 FEET (3,776 M), IT IS THE TALLEST MOUNTAIN IN THE NATION. IT IS WIDE AT THE BOTTOM, WITH A COVERING OF BRIGHT WHITE SNOW AND ICE ON TOP.

Mount Fuji stands about 70 miles (112 km) southwest of Tokyo, the capital of Japan. On clear days, people in Tokyo can see the mountain in the distance. The image of Mount Fuji rising above the surrounding countryside is a symbol of modern Japan. A picture of Mount Fuji appears on Japanese currency (paper money). Many Japanese books, travel posters, and paintings show pictures of the mountain.

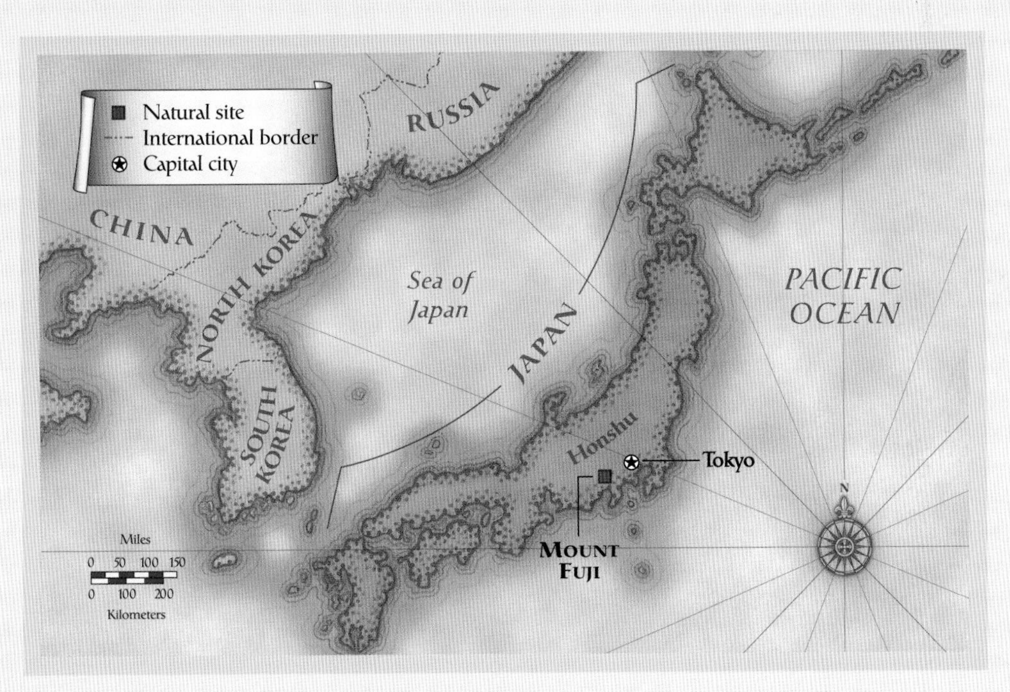

Right: *Young priests greet the rising sun at a temple on Mount Fuji's summit.* Below: *An eighteenth-century Japanese painting of Konohana Sakuya Hime, the goddess of Mount Fuji, shows the mountain standing between the moon and the sun.*

The name Mount Fuji is something of a mystery. *Fuji* might mean "eternal life" in an ancient Japanese language. Or the name might come from Huchi, an ancient Japanese god of fire. Historians aren't sure.

MOUNTAIN SPIRITS

More than one thousand years ago, the Japanese built a temple on top of Mount Fuji. The temple honored a beautiful mountain goddess. Her name, Konohana Sakuya Hime, means "blooming like the flowers of the trees." People said that the goddess floated above Mount Fuji in a cloud.

People climbed Mount Fuji to worship the goddess. They believed that only kind-hearted people should attempt the climb. Stories said that the goddess's helpers hid on Mount Fuji's summit. They watched for wicked climbers and threw them off the mountain.

Lo! There towers the lofty peak of Fuji
From between [the provinces of] Kai and
wave-washed Suruga,
The clouds of heaven dare not cross it,
Nor the birds of the air soar above it.
The snows quench the burning fires,
The fires consume the falling snow.
It baffles the tongue, it cannot be named
It is a spirit mysterious.

—Takahashi Mushimaro, a Japanese poet, circa A.D. 730

The town of Fujikawaguchiko lies at the foot of Mount Fuji, next to Lake Kawaguchi. The town is a popular vacation spot and a base for people who plan to climb the mountain.

In modern times, most Japanese people follow one of two religions: Shinto or Buddhism. Mount Fuji is sacred to both faiths. Both Shintoists and Buddhists believe that gods and spirits still live on the mountain. Many modern Japanese people climb the mountain to show respect to the gods and spirits.

Origin Stories

According to legend, Mount Fuji formed in 286 B.C. The story says that a woodcutter named Visu was going to bed one night. Suddenly, he heard a deep rumble, as if the ground underfoot was growling. His hut shook and began to break into pieces. Running outside, Visu was amazed to see a mountain rising out of the flat ground. The mountain got bigger and bigger. Eventually, it reached up into the clouds.

Scientists tell a different story about Mount Fuji's creation. They explain that

Lotus Mountain

Buddhists admire Mount Fuji because its peak looks like a lotus blossom. The lotus is special in Buddhism. Lotus plants live in ponds. Their roots grow in the mud. Their stems reach up through the water to form beautiful white blossoms. In Buddhism this path from mud to water to the sky symbolizes the human journey from earthly concerns to more spiritual ideas.

Climbers set off on a hike around the summit of Mount Fuji.

Above: *An aerial photograph shows the volcanic crater at Mount Fuji's summit.* Inset: *A high-speed train passes Mount Fuji. An eruption could destroy homes, roads, and train tracks.*

Mount Fuji has a volcano at its center. A volcano is an opening in Earth's surface. Sometimes, red-hot melted rock, gas, and ash from deep inside Earth erupt, or burst, through the opening. The volcano on Mount Fuji first erupted hundreds of thousands of years ago. Afterward, rock and ash from the eruption settled into a huge pile around the volcano. After more eruptions, the pile became a mountain.

LONG *Distance*

Winds can carry volcanic ash far through the air. When Mount Fuji erupted in 1707–1708, almost 6 inches (15 cm) of ash fell on Tokyo, 70 miles (112 km) away.

Steam escapes from cracks on the side of Mount Fuji. Scientists watch steam vents closely for signs of a new volcanic eruption.

Mount Fuji has erupted at least seventy-five times in the last 2,200 years. The mountain has grown higher and higher with each new eruption. The last eruption began on November 24, 1707. It lasted for two months.

Hot Spots

Japan is home to about 110 volcanoes. It is also the site of many earthquakes. Earthquakes and volcanoes occur where tectonic plates grind together. Japan is located along a line where the Eurasian Plate meets the Philippine Plate and the Pacific Plate.

Ever Wonder?

Does the United States have any active volcanoes? Yes. Mount Shasta in California, Mount Hood in Oregon, and Mount Saint Helens and Mount Rainier in Washington State are all active volcanoes. Mount Saint Helens last erupted in 1980. The eruption killed fifty-seven people and blasted a huge hole in the mountainside.

Scientists think that the Philippine Plate has a big gash directly beneath Mount Fuji. This gash, or hot spot, allows molten (melted) rock to rise up from deep below Earth's surface. The molten rock collects in a chamber below Mount Fuji. It sometimes bursts up through the volcano.

Worries about the Wonder

Although Mount Fuji looks peaceful, it is an active volcano. Active volcanoes are those that have erupted in the last few hundred years and will probably erupt again. A future eruption of Mount Fuji could cause a disaster in Japan.

Mount Fuji shadows the horizon behind Tokyo's skyline. If the volcano were to erupt, winds would carry ash all the way to Tokyo. The ash would coat streets and buildings.

FUJI'S *U.S. Sister*

Mount Rainier in Washington State is Mount Fuji's "sister" mountain. The two mountains look a lot alike. In 2003 private and government groups in the United States and Japan started the Sister Mountain Project. In this program, students from each country visit both mountains in summer. They learn about ways to preserve and protect the mountains.

For centuries, Japanese artists have considered Mount Fuji to be a symbol of symmetry and beauty. Ando Hiroshige made this woodcut of Mount Fuji in the 1850s.

It could kill people living nearby. It could damage roads, bridges, and buildings.

An eruption could also damage Mount Fuji's perfect looks. The mountain might explode during an eruption. Its top might fall off or its sides might collapse.

Scientists are watching Mount Fuji closely. They have placed scientific instruments on the mountain. These instruments can detect rumblings and other warning signs of an eruption. If an eruption seems likely, scientists will warn people to evacuate, or leave the area.

"The most beautiful sight in Japan, and certainly one of the most beautiful mountains in the world, is the distant [view] of Fuji on cloudless days."

—Greek American writer Lafcadio Hearn, a specialist on Japanese culture, 1898

Above: *Volunteers remove trash from Mount Fuji.* Inset: *Hundreds of hikers crowd the shrine at the summit of Mount Fuji. As the number of visitors increases, it becomes harder to keep the mountain clean.*

People are another threat to Mount Fuji. Every summer, almost five hundred thousand people climb on the mountain slopes. Many people climb all the way to the top. Some climbers leave behind toilet paper, empty bottles, and other trash. Environmental groups are working to clean up the mess. They ask people not to leave trash on Mount Fuji. The Japanese government also protects Mount Fuji. The mountain is part of a national park, created in 1936.

4 Sumatra Rain Forests

A river winds through the rain forest on the northern end of the island of Sumatra. Because forest trees and plants grow so close together, it is easier to travel on the river than to travel on land.

In the 1600s, a Dutch doctor named Jacob de Bondt visited Sumatra, an island in modern-day Indonesia in Southeast Asia. De Bondt was surprised to see a strange animal in the rain forest. It looked like a wild woman with long red hair. The local people already had a name for this animal. They called it an orangutan. That name means "man of the forest" in the Malay language. De Bondt wrote about orangutans in a scientific book. That's how people around the world first learned about this fascinating creature.

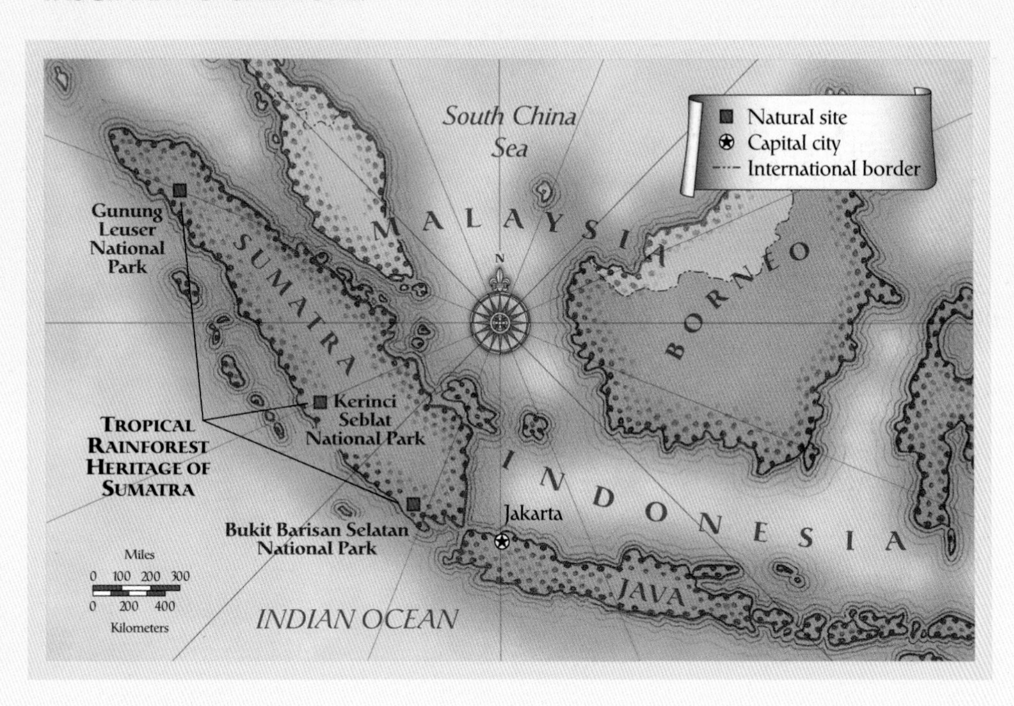

Great Apes

Orangutans are part of the great ape family. This group also includes bonobos, chimpanzees, and gorillas. Orangutans are the only great apes that live outside Africa. Orangutans are bigger than bonobos and chimps but smaller than gorillas. An adult male orangutan stands about 53 inches (135 cm) tall and weighs about 200 pounds (91 kg).

Orangutans spend most of their lives in treetops. They use their long, curving fingers and toes to grasp branches. They swing gracefully from tree to tree as they travel through the forest. They are clumsy and awkward when walking on the ground, however.

Orangutans are mainly vegetarians. They eat mostly fruit, seeds, leaves, flowers, and bark. They occasionally eat insects, birds' eggs, birds, and other small animals. Orangutans don't have to leave the treetops to find water. They sip rainwater that collects on leaves and in the crooks between tree branches.

An orangutan grazes on tree leaves in the Sumatra rain forest. Long arms help orangutans swing through the trees.

Most orangutans live thirty-five to forty-five years. They do not live in big groups. Young orangutans live with their mothers for about three years. Adult males live alone.

"This curious monster with its human face does exist as it has the human habit of sighing."

—Jacob de Bondt, describing an orangutan, 1642

Left: *A female orangutan keeps watch over her baby.* Below: *Thick forests provide plenty of food for orangutans.*

Males and females spend time together only when they mate. Females give birth to one baby at a time. They have a new baby about every three years.

Orangutans are very strong. But they are gentle. They do not attack large animals. They become aggressive only when they need to defend themselves.

Homelands

Orangutans once lived in tropical rain forests throughout southern China and Southeast Asia. They numbered about three hundred thousand in 1900. In the twentieth century, people began to cut down the forests where orangutans live. People also

Above: *The Alas River winds through Gunung Leuser National Park.* Inset: *Orangutans visit a feeding station at a center for injured orangutans at the edge of Gunung Leuser National Park.*

captured orangutans and locked them up in zoos. Some people even hunted orangutans for food. Orangutans could no longer travel freely or live peacefully in their natural homes. Their numbers began to decline.

In the twenty-first century, orangutans live only in two places. One is the island of Sumatra in Indonesia. The other is the island of Borneo. Borneo is divided among the nations of Brunei, Malaysia, and Indonesia. Scientists think that fewer than fifty thousand wild orangutans are left on these two islands.

Rain Forest Neighbors

Rain forests are woodlands with tall trees and lots of rain. Tropical rain forests are warm year-round. Sumatra has the perfect ingredients for the growth of tropical rain forests. The temperature there averages 80°F (27°C) all year. The island gets between 90 and 185 inches (229 and 470 cm) of rain per year. Sumatra's soil is very fertile. Dense forests grow easily there.

Sumatra's rain forests provide a home for a wide variety of animals. In addition to orangutans, Sumatran tigers and Asian elephants live in the rain forest. More than 250,000 kinds of insects live there. Thousands of birds and fish live there too. Some rain forest animals are rare. They are found nowhere else on Earth. One is the two-horned Sumatran rhinoceros. Only three hundred to five hundred of these animals remain in the world.

The rain forest is home to more than ten thousand kinds of plants. Some are quite unique. For instance, the fruit of the durian tree tastes sweet, but it smells like stinky socks. Bengal bamboo trees may grow as

A Sumatran tiger hunts in the rain forest. Sumatran tigers are the smallest of all living tigers.

Big *Stinker*

The titan arum *(below)* is a plant that grows wild only in the rain forests of Sumatra. It can grow to be 6 feet (2 m) high. The plant's flower looks pretty, but it smells terrible! In fact, people sometimes call it the corpse flower because it smells like a dead animal. For the plant, the stink is useful. It attracts flies, which pollinate the flower—helping the plant reproduce.

tall as an eight-story building. Tualang trees are also tall trees. Honeybees build hives in their branches. Some tualang trees have one hundred hives. Each hive contains up to thirty thousand bees.

Spice Islands

About seventeen thousand islands belong to Indonesia. They sit between the Pacific Ocean to the northeast and the Indian Ocean to the southwest. People have lived in Indonesia for thousands of years. The first inhabitants came from the Asian mainland. They probably arrived in boats from India, China, Vietnam, and other places.

In ancient times, merchants from India, Arabia, and China traded with people from Indonesia. Later, merchants from Europe also traveled to Indonesia. The traders sailed to Indonesia to buy cloves, nutmeg, and other spices. The spices were highly prized in Europe. Parts of Indonesia became known as the Spice Islands.

In modern times, about 230 million people live in Indonesia. It has the fourth-largest population of any country on Earth (after China, India, and the United States). More than 40 million people live on Sumatra. Many of them work in cities. Others work on farms that produce rice, corn, tea, rubber, coffee, coconuts, palm oil, and spices.

Pricy Spices

In ancient times, spices from Indonesia were expensive and hard to get. In places such as ancient Greece and Rome, people used spices to keep food from spoiling and as medicine. Rich women sometimes wore lockets of fragrant cloves *(below)* to cover unpleasant smells. People also chewed cloves to freshen their breath.

Workers plant rice on a farm on Sumatra.

Above: *Sunlight breaks through clouds above the Sumatra rain forest.* Below: *Some parts of the Sumatra rain forest are peat forests. These dense, swampy forests grow on layers of partly decomposed leaves and wood. Farmers damage this type of forest by draining its water and converting the land to farm fields.*

Right: *Sumatran lumber workers load felled trees onto trucks in the rain forest.* Below: *A logging road and canal cut through the rain forest in northeastern Sumatra. Loggers use canals to float logs to processing plants.*

WORRIES ABOUT THE WONDER

Sumatra's rain forests are disappearing. People have cut down rain forest trees to make room for farms, towns, and roads. They have also cut trees for lumber. Between 2000 and 2005, loggers cut down about 300 acres (121 hectares) of forest every hour. (That's about the size of three hundred high school football fields.)

The government of Indonesia has passed laws that forbid cutting down trees in rain forests. However, people often ignore the laws. As the rain forests disappear, orangutans and other forest animals have fewer places to live. Some animals have become extinct, or died out altogether. Other animals, such as orangutans, are in danger of extinction.

"Almost all of the . . . rainforest has been logged to some extent in the last 60 years and some of its species have been staring extinction in the face."

—Graham Wynne, Royal Society for the Protection of Birds, 2007

Sumatrans sort through the ruins of businesses in the northern city of Banda Aceh after a tsunami hit Indonesia in 2004.

DOUBLE *Disaster*

On December 26, 2004, an earthquake hit underwater near the coast of Sumatra. The quake caused huge tsunamis. These giant waves of water crashed onto the land. The waves killed more than 100,000 people on Sumatra and another 130,000 people in other places. The waves also destroyed people's homes. The tsunamis did not reach Sumatra's tropical rain forests. But they wound up causing great damage to those forests anyway. People left homeless by the tsunamis needed wood to build new homes. They bought the wood from loggers who illegally cut down trees in the rain forest.

To protect the rain forests, in the 1980s and 1990s, the Indonesian government created three national parks: Gunung Leuser National Park, Kerinci Seblat National Park, and Bukit Barisan Selatan National Park. The parks provide a safe home for orangutans and other wild animals. In 2004 UNESCO named these parks the Tropical Rainforest Heritage of Sumatra. They became a World Heritage Site.

5 The Dead Sea

Shallow waters on the coast of the Dead Sea reflect the blue sky. Salt crystals from the water build up on rocks and heaps of sand, creating white patterns on the shore.

In a swimming pool or at the beach, it takes work to stay on top of the water. If you don't know how to float or swim, you'll sink. In the Dead Sea between Israel and Jordan, it is almost impossible to sink. You can wade into the sea, sit down, and float on the water as if resting on an air mattress. You can even read a book in the sea without getting it wet.

The Dead Sea is not a real sea. It is actually a large lake—only about 50 miles (81 km) long and 10 miles (16 km) wide. But people call it a sea because it is salty like seawater—very, very salty. It is the salt in the Dead Sea that allows people to float in the water instead of sinking.

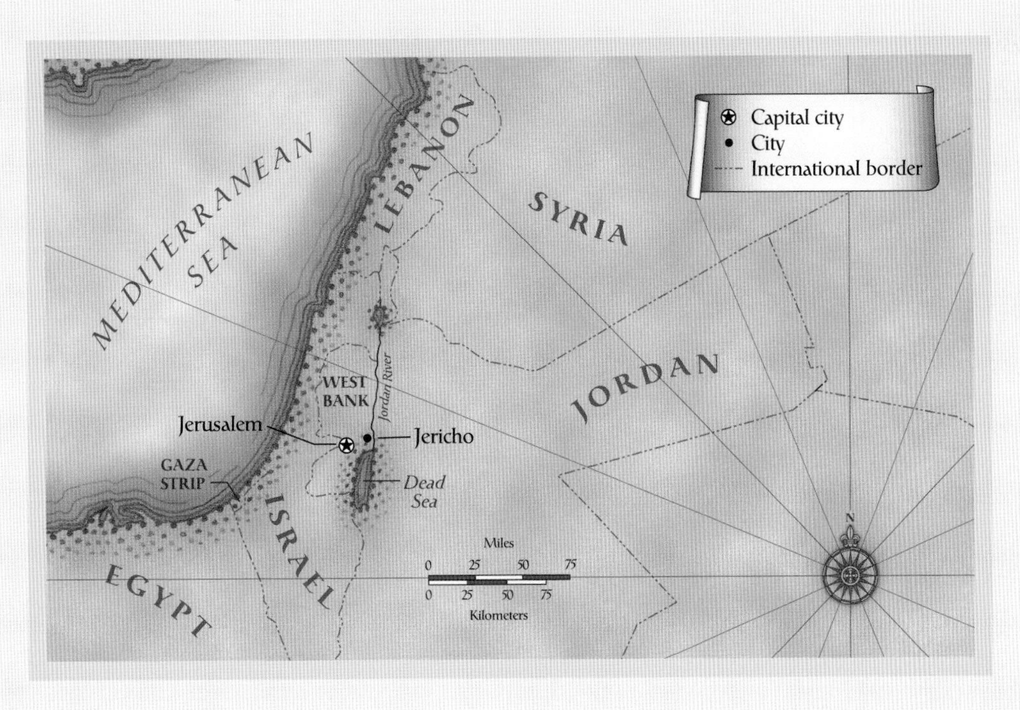

Heavy on the Salt

Anyone who has accidentally gotten a gulp of water at an ocean beach knows that ocean water is salty. Water in the Dead Sea is about nine times saltier than ocean water. If you filled up a milk jug with Dead Sea water, about one-third of the jug would contain salt.

Salt water is denser, or heavier, than freshwater. The heavier the water, the easier it is to float in it. Imagine getting into a swimming pool. In getting in, you displace, or push aside, a certain amount of water. If that amount of water weighs less than you do, you will sink. If that amount of water weighs more

How Low Can You Go?

The shore around the Dead Sea is the lowest land on Earth. It sits about 1,310 feet (399 m) below sea level. The very bottom of the sea, in the deepest part, is about 2,600 feet (792 m) below sea level.

Swimmers float in the Dead Sea. The water is so dense (heavy) that it is easy to float in it, even when a person is wearing clothes.

Left: *A visitor reads while floating on the surface of the Dead Sea. Boats cannot sail on the Dead Sea because they would float so high on the dense water that they would tip over.*

Large salt crystals cover rocks on the coast of the Dead Sea in Jordan.

than you do, you will float. In the Dead Sea, the salty water a person displaces always weighs more than that person. So people never sink in the Dead Sea. They bob on the surface.

Recipe for a Salty Lake

The Dead Sea formed millions of years ago when two tectonic plates spread apart. The moving plates opened up a gigantic crack in Earth's surface. Known as the Great Rift Valley, the crack extends for 4,500 miles (7,200 km), from Syria in the Middle East to Mozambique in southern Africa.

The sun sets over the Dead Sea. This aerial photograph shows the salt deposits that extend up the shore from the edge of the water.

Water from the Mediterranean Sea flooded part of the valley. The water from the sea was salty. Later, the tectonic plates moved again. This time they created highlands that blocked the valley from the Mediterranean Sea. The salty water remained trapped in the valley. It had become a salty lake—the Dead Sea.

"There is a lake . . . such that if you bind a man or beast and throw it in it floats and does not sink."

—Greek philosopher Aristotle, mid-300s B.C.

More Minerals

In addition to salt, the Dead Sea contains large amounts of magnesium, potash, and other minerals. Companies dig up the minerals, which are used to make machinery, fertilizers, and other products.

The Dead Sea is surrounded by desert. Only about 2 inches (5 cm) of rain fall on the area each year. Temperatures in the summer often reach 102°F (39°C). The Jordan River and other small rivers flow into the Dead Sea. These rivers are mostly freshwater, with only a little salt. But in the desert heat, the freshwater evaporates (dries up) quickly. Only the salt remains behind.

Over time, as water has evaporated, more and more salt has built up in the Dead Sea. Salt deposits cover the sea bottom. Salt has piled up like snowdrifts along the shores.

Salt deposits trap small pools of water on the shore of the Dead Sea. The water in these pools evaporates (dries up) quickly, leaving still more salt behind.

Life at the Dead Sea

People first settled around the Dead Sea at least eleven thousand years ago. Archaeologists have found the ruins of ancient villages and cities near the sea. One of these ancient villages is Jericho, on the west bank of the Jordan River. People still live in Jericho. Experts say it is the oldest continuously inhabited city in the world. People have lived in Jericho since at least 8000 B.C.

In ancient times, people had different names for the Dead Sea. The ancient Greeks called it Lake Asphaltites. That name came from asphalt that seeps up from the bottom of the sea to the water's

About 50 B.C., rulers of a Jewish kingdom built these baths as part of a palace near Jericho.

surface. Asphalt is similar to tar. The ancient Greeks and Romans used asphalt from the Dead Sea to seal cracks in their ships. The ancient Egyptians used it like glue to fasten the strips of cloth wrapped around mummies.

No large plants or animals can live in the salty water of the Dead Sea. It appears to be a dead zone. That's how the name Dead Sea came about. Unlucky fish that wash into the Dead Sea from the Jordan River quickly die.

But the Dead Sea is not really dead. In 1936 scientists discovered that bacteria and other microscopic creatures live in the Dead Sea. These organisms have adapted to the salty water that kills other living things. Scientists named the

DEAD SEA *Scrolls*

In 1947 local people discovered three ancient scrolls in a cave near the Dead Sea. Later, people found hundreds of additional "Dead Sea Scrolls." The scrolls contain ancient writings. Some of them are texts from the Bible *(below)*. Others are legal documents and literary works. The scrolls were written between about 250 B.C. and A.D. 68. They offer great amounts of information about life in the ancient Middle East.

Salt deposits on the shoreline in Jordan show the Dead Sea's shrinking water level.

creatures halophiles. That name comes from two Greek words that mean "salt loving."

Healthy Sea

The Dead Sea was one of the world's first health resorts. In ancient times, people from Egypt, Rome, and Greece visited the sea. They came to enjoy the hot, dry weather and to bathe in the warm, salty water.

In modern times, the Dead Sea is still a healing center. Spas and resorts line its shores. Some people say that the salty water relieves arthritis and other ailments. Others say that mud from the Dead Sea is good for your skin. Many people like to season their food with salt from the Dead Sea.

Worries about the Wonder

The Dead Sea is drying up. Since the mid-1900s, the sea has shrunk by almost one-third. Its water level drops almost 2 feet (0.6 m) every year. The sea is shrinking because its water evaporates faster than new water flows in from the Jordan and other rivers. People are mainly to blame. They take a lot of water from the Jordan River to use for drinking and farming.

The governments of Jordan, Israel, and the Palestinian territories (West Bank, Gaza Strip, and East Jerusalem) are working to preserve the Dead Sea. They are talking about building the Two Seas Canal. If the canal is built, it will carry water from the Red Sea to the Dead Sea. The Red Sea, south of Israel and Jordan, has plenty of water for this.

6 Cappadocia

Tall rock towers rise from a valley floor in Cappadocia, Turkey. These are the "fairy chimneys" described by traveler Paul Lucas in the 1700s.

In the early 1700s, Frenchman Paul Lucas visited Turkey. He was in charge of a French government expedition to explore the Middle East. In 1712 Lucas published a book about his travels. In this book, he described a place called Cappadocia in central Turkey.

According to Lucas, Cappadocia was amazing. It was filled with huge towers of stone. Lucas called them fairy chimneys. Some of them looked like pyramids, lions, birds, and mushrooms. Others looked like people wearing hats. Still others resembled mothers cradling babies in their arms. Some of the stone formations had beautiful colors: green, blue, yellow, and red.

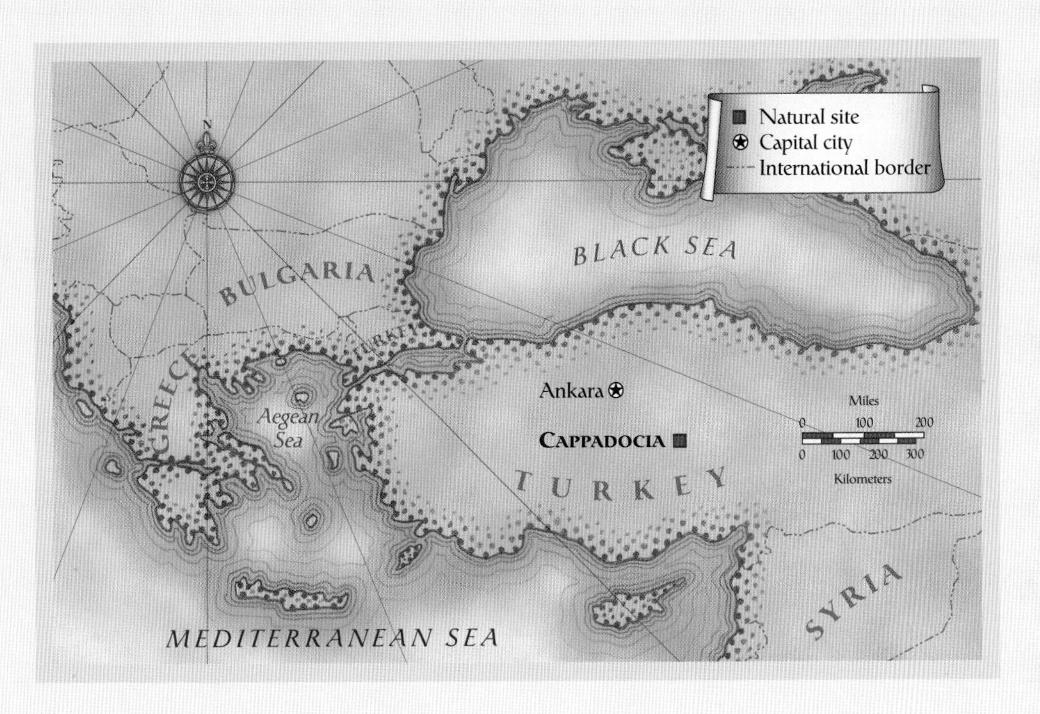

"Here stood countless [stone towers]. . . . Each of these formations possessed a beautiful door, a charming staircase by which to gain entrance and large windows in all the rooms. . . . They numbered not several hundreds, but more than a couple of thousand."

—Paul Lucas, on visiting Cappadocia, 1712

Lucas also wrote about mansions carved out of stone. The dwellings had beautifully carved doorways, windows, rooms, and stairways.

At first, some people didn't believe Lucas's story. Cappadocia sounded too fantastic to be real. But later travelers confirmed Lucas's description. He had discovered one of the most fascinating natural wonders of the Middle East.

Below: ***Natural processes shaped this formation in Cappadocia's Goreme Valley before humans added their own carvings.*** **Inset:** ***This door leads to a police call box in a Cappadocian town.***

Left: *Turkey's Mount Erciyes is one of the volcanoes that shaped Cappadocia.* Below: *Erosion created these leaf shapes in a Cappadocian valley.*

Creation

Cappadocia's history goes back millions of years. The area around Cappadocia has many volcanoes. Scientists think the volcanoes began erupting about 70 million years ago. Ash and rock from the eruptions collected around the volcanoes. It piled up into cone-shaped mountains.

The mountains were made of different kinds of rocks. On the outside was ignimbrite rock. This rock is light and crumbly. Beneath the ignimbrite rock was a harder kind of rock. Over thousands of years, wind, rain, floods, and rivers wore away the soft ignimbrite rock, exposing the harder rock underneath. This erosion, or wearing away, created Cappadocia's fairy chimneys.

As rainwater collected in this low area of Cappadocia, it washed away soft parts of the rock, exposing these colorful formations.

INCREDIBLE IGNIMBRITE

As the ignimbrite rock crumbled, it settled on the ground around Cappadocia. It turned into rich, fertile soil—perfect for growing crops. Thousands of years ago, ancient people discovered the fertile soil. They settled in Cappadocia. They started to grow grapes, wheat, apricots, onions, and other food. Eventually, they built villages around their farms.

Often, when people build houses and towns, they use the materials at hand. They cut down trees to make boards. They dig clay to make bricks. They stack up rocks to make walls.

An artist living in Cappadocia in the 1800s B.C. made this lion-shaped jar.

Comfy *Caves*

Some caves are cold and damp. But the caves of Cappadocia are comfy. That's because of the ignimbrite rock. The rock is filled with air pockets that trap warm air. They help keep the caves dry and warm year-round.

The people at Cappadocia didn't have to go to all this trouble. They discovered that they could carve right into the soft ignimbrite rock of nearby cliffs and hills. People could also carve into the cone-shaped fairy chimneys.

By carving into the rock, the ancient people of Cappadocia created enormous cave towns. Some towns were six or seven levels high, extending up the side of a cliff or mountain. Some were cut 250 feet (76 m) deep into sides of cliffs.

Humans carved dozens of apartments and tunnels into this rock formation in Uchisar, a town in Cappadocia. The tower is the highest point in the area. In times of war, people took shelter in this natural fortress, which was easy to defend against attackers.

Ancient Living *in the Modern World*

In modern times, some people still live in underground homes in Cappadocia. Some farmers use the underground chambers to store grain, fruits, and vegetables.

Left: *People still occupy cave homes in Cappadocia.* Top: *Women dry apricots on the roof of their Cappadocian home.* Above: *This cave home has one large room with several shelves and storage areas, as well as a rock that may have been used as a table.*

Residents of Cappadocia's Ihlara Valley cut this massive church out of the face of a cliff. Many of the churches in this area included storage areas, rooms for monks and other church staff, and even graveyards.

YUMMY *Yufka*

Bakers in Cappadocia make thin flat bread called *yufka*. The loaves look like big pancakes. They are about 18 inches (46 cm) wide. In past eras, bakers sometimes made a whole year's supply of yufka at one time. They placed the bread in carved-rock storage chambers. Because the air was so dry, the bread stayed fresh for almost one year. Before eating the dried yufka, people sprinkled it with water to soften it.

The towns had wells for drawing water, fireplaces for cooking, chimneys to let out smoke, and shafts to let in air and sunlight. People built special rooms for making wine, grinding grain, and sheltering animals. Tunnels and passageways connected the rooms. Longer tunnels connected one town to another.

DEFENSE

The underground towns not only provided shelter. They also provided

Right: *Monks painted elaborate frescoes (wall paintings) on the ceilings of Cappadocian cave churches.*
Below: *Travelers in Cappadocia may never see some of the area's homes from the road.*

protection. In ancient times, different empires fought to control Turkey and the surrounding lands. Often, invading armies attacked villagers, killed people, and stole their possessions.

But Cappadocia's towns were hidden inside mountains. Doorways were tucked out of sight. Often, armies passing through the area did not even notice the towns.

In the A.D. 100s, the Christian religion was brand new. Roman rulers punished Christians for their beliefs. Some Christians fled to Cappadocia. They were able to live there safely in towns hidden inside the mountains. The early Christians created beautiful churches inside their hidden towns. They decorated the walls and ceilings with paintings.

"Nature had never displayed herself to the foreign observer's eye in such an extraordinary fashion. I have never heard of a more long-lived and dream-like natural phenomenon in any other region of the world."

—French traveler Charles Texier, describing Cappadocia, 1862

Protecting Cappadocia

In modern times, Cappadocia is one of the most popular tourist attractions in Turkey. Every year, thousands of visitors come to see the fairy chimneys and other cave buildings. Visitors can tour inside the buildings. Some buildings have even been turned into hotels and restaurants. Cappadocia is part of the Goreme National Park. In 1985 UNESCO named this park a World Heritage Site.

Visitors to Cappadocia can stay in hotels like this one, which rents out rooms carved out of the rock. Money from tourism helps to maintain the region. But the increasing number of visitors could damage the fragile rock.

7 The Chocolate Hills

The sun rises over the Chocolate Hills on the island of Bohol, Philippines. As the seasons change, these hills change from brown to green and back again.

DO YOU LIKE TO EAT CHOCOLATE KISSES? IMAGINE MORE THAN ONE THOUSAND GIANT CHOCOLATE KISSES, AS TALL AS BIG BUILDINGS. THAT'S WHAT YOU'LL SEE IF YOU VISIT THE CHOCOLATE HILLS IN THE PHILIPPINES. UNFORTUNATELY FOR CANDY LOVERS, THE HILLS AREN'T REALLY MADE OF CHOCOLATE. THE ONLY CHOCOLATE IN THE HILLS IS IN THE NAME. BUT THE CHOCOLATE HILLS ARE STILL WONDERFUL.

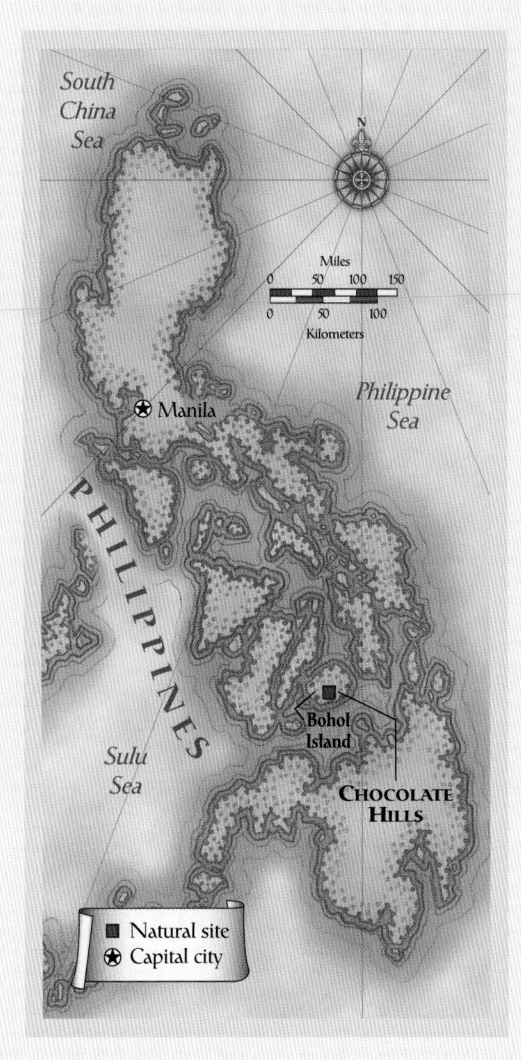

The Philippines is a nation in Southeast Asia. It is made up of about 7,100 islands in the western Pacific Ocean. If all those islands were pushed together, they would form an area about the size of the U.S. state of Arizona.

"Most people who first see pictures of this landscape can hardly believe that these hills are not . . . man-made."

—Philippine photographer Salvador Andre, 2007

The Chocolate Hills are located on Bohol, one of the Philippine Islands. The hills have become the symbol of Bohol. Their picture appears on Bohol's flag.

Chocolate Brown

The Chocolate Hills are mounds of soil and rock. During Bohol's rainy season, from July to November, the Chocolate Hills are green. They are covered by thick carpets of grass. During the dry season, from December to June, the grass dies. The hills turn a chocolate brown color.

Green vegetation covers the Chocolate Hills during the rainy season. Grasses and ferns grow well on the steep stone slopes.

The sun rises over the Chocolate Hills. Palm trees and rice fields fill the valleys between the hills.

The hills are clustered together in an area of about 19 square miles (50 sq. km). There are 1,268 hills in all. Some of them are cone shaped. They are wide at the bottom and rise to a narrow peak. Other hills have a dome shape. They look like halves of huge soccer balls rising out of the ground. Some of the hills are almost as tall as a forty-story building.

Making Chocolate

According to one legend, the hills were formed when two giants had a fight on Bohol. For days, the giants threw boulders and dirt at each other. Finally, the giants got tired, made friends, and left Bohol. But they left the island littered with enormous boulders—the Chocolate Hills. Another legend says that a giant named Arogo cried over the death of a friend. His tears dried up to form the Chocolate Hills.

Modern scientists disagree about how the Chocolate Hills formed. Some scientists think that undersea volcanoes splattered huge blobs of molten rock on Bohol. The blobs hardened into big mounds. Over the centuries, rain and wind smoothed the mounds into the neatly shaped Chocolate Hills. Other scientists think the hills began as blocks of stone buried inside softer clay.

They say that rain and wind wore away the clay and smoothed the stone into mounds.

People of the Hills

People have lived on Bohol and other islands in the Philippines for more than twenty-five thousand years. Scientists think that the first inhabitants arrived from the Asian mainland.

The first inhabitants left no written records. Instead, they passed down stories from one generation to another. Stories say that around A.D. 1200, people came to Bohol from the distant island of Mindanao. They built a village on stilts in the water between Bohol and the island of Panglao. The village grew into a powerful civilization called the kingdom of Dapitan.

For many years, the Philippines were controlled by Spain. The Spanish named the islands for a Spanish prince, Philip, who later became King Philip II.

Ever Wonder?

How did Bohol get its name? People have two different theories. First, the name might come from a local word that means "hole." Bohol has a lot of caves. Those might be the "holes" that led to the name. Another explanation says that *Bohol* means "a hole that gushes water." The island has plenty of those kinds of holes as well. They are natural springs, openings in the ground and rocks where water pours out.

Traditional Filipino houses like this one on Bohol rest on stilts. This building technique protects homes from floods during the rainy season.

Left: *A woman plants rice in a field in the Chocolate Hills region.* Below: *Farmers build houses and plant crops at the base of the Chocolate Hills.*

THE UNITED STATES' *Chocolate Hills*

The United States once ruled Bohol and the rest of the Philippines. Spain gave the United States control of the Philippines in 1899, after the Spanish-American War (1898). The United States granted independence to the Philippines in 1946.

Spanish merchants bought spices from India, China, and other Asian countries. They sailed with the spices to Europe and the Americas. They used the Philippines as a stopping-off point on their long sea voyages. The Spanish also introduced aspects of European culture, such as the Spanish language and the Catholic religion, to the Philippines.

Above: *Thick forest surrounds some of the Chocolate Hills.* Inset: *Students visit a tourist center in the Chocolate Hills.*

In modern times, the Philippines is an independent nation. It is home to almost 90 million people. Manila is the capital city. On Bohol some people work as farmers. They raise rice, coconut, and corn. Other people make a living by fishing in the waters around Bohol. Still other people work in shops, offices, and other businesses.

"The fame of the Chocolate Hills is not only known in this country but worldwide."

—Philippine president Gloria Macapagal-Arroyo, 2003

Eyeing the *Tarsier*

Primates are animals that see well with two eyes, use their hands and feet to grasp things, and have large brains. Humans are primates, and so are monkeys and gorillas. The world's smallest primate lives in the forests around the Chocolate Hills and in other places in Southeast Asia. It is a monkeylike creature named the Bohol tarsier *(below)*. It is small enough to fit in the palm of an adult man's hand. Large tarsiers weigh only about 6 ounces (160 grams).

Compared to their tiny bodies, tarsiers have huge eyes and fingers. Tarsiers can turn their heads 180 degrees—that's half of a circle. They eat crickets and other insects. The tarsier is an endangered species. That means its numbers are shrinking. It might soon become extinct. The Philippine government has established a preserve on Bohol to protect these creatures.

Worries about the Wonder

The Chocolate Hills are one of the most popular tourist attractions in the Philippines. Thousands of people visit the area each year to marvel at this natural wonder.

Many tourists visit the Chocolate Hills Complex. It is a resort and recreation center built on two of the hills. At the complex, people can climb more than two hundred steps to an observation deck. From there, they can view the other hills. The resort also has a children's play area, a swimming pool, a restaurant, a hotel, and other attractions.

To protect this natural wonder, in 1988 the Philippine government declared the Chocolate Hills to be a national geological monument. Government rules prevent people from using the hills in ways that could spoil their natural beauty. People cannot buy individual hills, build houses on top of them, or place billboards there. The government wants to protect this natural wonder for many future generations.

Timeline

ca. 8000 B.C.	People establish the town of Jericho near the Dead Sea.
mid-400s B.C.	The Greek historian Herodotus makes the first "seven wonders" list.
ca. 250 B.C.–A.D. 68	People create manuscripts called the Dead Sea Scrolls.
A.D. 100s	Early Christians flee to Cappadocia to practice their religion freely.
ca. 1275	Marco Polo travels through the Gobi Desert as part of a larger journey through China and central Asia.
early 1600s	Jacob de Bondt sees an orangutan in the Sumatra rain forest. He later writes about the animal in a scientific book.
1707–1708	Mount Fuji has its most recent eruption. The eruption drops almost 6 inches (15 cm) of ash on Tokyo.
1712	French traveler Paul Lucas writes about his visit to Cappadocia.
1823	British geographer and engineer George Everest begins to survey India and the Himalaya mountains.
1852	Andrew Scott Waugh measures Mount Everest. He determines that it is the tallest mountain in the world.
1923	U.S. scientist Roy Chapman Andrews discovers the bones of a dinosaur in the Gobi Desert. He calls the dinosaur *Oviraptor*.
1936	Scientists discover that bacteria and other microbes live in the Dead Sea. The Japanese government creates a national park to protect Mount Fuji.
1947	People discover the first of the Dead Sea Scrolls.
1953	Mountain climbers Edmund Hillary and Tenzing Norgay become the first people to reach the summit of Mount Everest.
1976	Nepal creates Sagarmatha National Park in the area around Mount Everest.
1979	Sagarmatha National Park becomes a World Heritage Site.
1985	Cappadocia becomes a World Heritage Site.
1988	The government of the Philippines designates the Chocolate Hills as a national geological monument.
2003	The Japanese and Americans begin the Sister Mountain Project to study and protect Mount Fuji and Mount Rainier.
2004	The Tropical Rainforest Heritage of Sumatra becomes a World Heritage Site. Tsunamis kill more than one hundred thousand people on Sumatra.
2008	In a lead-up to the Olympic Games, climbers carry the Olympic torch to the top of Mount Everest.

Choose an Eighth Wonder

Now that you've read about the seven natural wonders of Asia and the Middle East, do a little research to choose an eighth wonder. You may enjoy working with a friend.

To do your research, look at some of the websites and books listed on pages 76 and 77. Look for places in Asia and the Middle East that

- ***are especially large***
- ***are exceptionally beautiful***
- ***were unknown to foreigners for many centuries***
- ***are unlike any other place on Earth***

You might even try gathering photos and writing your own chapter on the eighth wonder!

Glossary and Pronunciation Guide

altitude: height above sea level

Bohol: boh-HAHL

Cappadocia: ka-puh-DOH-shuh

Chomolungma: choh-moh-LUNG-muh

continents: the seven giant landmasses on Earth. The continents are Africa, Antarctica, Asia, Australia, Europe, North America, and South America.

desert: a dry land that receives less than 10 inches (25 cm) of rain or snow each year

desertification: the process of fertile land turning into desert

endangered species: a plant or animal species that is in danger of dying out

erode: to wear away. Wind, rain, rivers, and other natural processes cause most erosion of rock and soil.

extinction: when all the members of a plant or animal species have died out

Gobi: GOH-bee

grazing: allowing livestock such as sheep and goats to feed on plants

Himalayas: hih-muh-LAY-uhz

ignimbrite: ihg-nehm-BRYT

mirage: an optical illusion, often caused by heat. In the desert, a mirage might look like a pool of water or a person, when in fact nothing is there.

Nepal: nay-PAHL

rain forest: a forest in a region that receives at least 100 inches (254 cm) of rain each year. Tropical rain forests are rain forests that grow in hot places.

Sagarmatha: sah-gahr-MAH-tah

Sherpa: SHEHR-puh

Sumatra: soo-MAH-truh

summit: the highest point of a mountain

surveyor: a person who measures the size and boundaries of land formations

tarsier: TAHR-see-uhr

tectonic plates: giant slabs of rock that form Earth's crust

tsunami: soo-NAH-mee

volcano: an opening in Earth's surface through which ash, gases, and melted rock occasionally burst forth

Source Notes

13 Richard C. Blum, Erica Stone, and Coburn Broughton, eds., *Himalaya: Personal Stories of Grandeur, Challenge, and Hope* (Washington, DC: National Geographic, 2006), 246.

15 Alpine Ascents International, "Why Everest?" *Alpine Ascents International,* 2007, http://www.alpineascents.com/why-climb-everest.asp (December 19, 2007).

18 Silkroad Foundation, "Marco Polo and His Travels," *silk-road.com,* 2000, http://www.silk-road.com/artl/marcopolo.shtml (November 13, 2007).

20 Robin Hanbury-Tenison, *The Oxford Book of Exploration* (Oxford: Oxford University Press, 1993), 3.

29 "Fuji," *Earlywomenmasters.net,* 2006, http://www.earlywomenmasters.net/masters/fuji/index.html (December 19, 2007).

34 Lafcadio Hern, *Fuji-No-Yama,* December 12, 1898, http://www.eldritchpress.org/lh/fuji.html (November 12, 2007).

38 Donald F. Lach, "Asia in the Eyes of Europe: Sixteenth through Eighteenth Centuries," *University of Chicago Library,* 1991, http://www.lib.uchicago.edu/e/su/southasia/lach.html (December 19, 2007).

44 Michael McCarthy, "Paradise Lost—and Regained," *Independent* (London), April 3, 2007, 12.

50 "Meteorology by Aristotle," *Internet Classics Archive,* September 13, 2007, http://classics.mit.edu/Aristotle/meteorology.2.ii.html (December 19, 2007).

56 "Belle Cappadoce," *Mephisto Voyages,* 2005, http://www.mephistovoyage.com/information/fr_cappadocia.htm (November 28, 2007).

63 Ibid.

66 "Learn about the World through Photography: The Chocolate Hills," *Trek Earth,* 2007, http://www.trekearth.com/gallery/Asia/Philippines/photo793456.htm (December 19, 2007).

70 *Asia Journal,* "Move Over, Boracay; Panglao Island Beckons," November 5, 2003, http://www.asianjournal.com/cgi-bin/view_info.cgi?code=1827 (December 19, 2007).

Selected Bibliography

Allan, Tony, and Andrew Warren, eds. *Deserts: The Encroaching Wilderness.* New York: Oxford University Press, 1993.

Cleare, John. *Mountains of the World.* San Diego: Thunder Bay Press, 1997.

Collins, Mark, ed. *The Last Rain Forests: A World Conservation Atlas.* New York: Oxford University Press, 1990.

Flegg, Jim. *Deserts: Miracle of Life.* New York: Facts on File, 1993.

Hanbury-Tenison, Robin. *The Oxford Book of Exploration.* Oxford: Oxford University Press, 1993.

Hancock, Paul, and Brian J. Skinner, eds. *The Oxford Companion to the Earth.* Oxford: Oxford University Press, 2000.

Krakauer, Jon. *Into Thin Air: A Personal Account of the Mount Everest Disaster.* New York: Anchor Books, 1997.

Kropf, John W. *Unknown Sands: Journeys around the World's Most Isolated Country.* Houston, TX: Dusty Sparks Publications, 2006.

Luhr, James F., ed. *Earth.* London: Dorling Kindersley, 2003.

Man, John, and Chris Schuler. *The Traveler's Atlas.* Hauppage, NY: Barron's Educational Services, 1998.

Further Reading and Websites

Brazil, Mark. *Wild Asia: Spirit of a Continent.* Gretna, LA: Pelican Publishing Company, 2000. Wild Asia presents incredible photographs of the homes of the animals, plants, and insects that live on the world's largest continent. Brief captions help explain the area's great diversity.

Dickinson, Matt. *The Other Side of Everest: Climbing the North Face through the Killer Storm.* New York: Random House, 1999. Filmmaker Matt Dickinson tells the story of his expedition to Mount Everest in 1996. His group was among ten different groups attempting to climb the mountain at the same time. Twelve climbers died in the quest.

Goldstein, Margaret J. *Israel in Pictures.* Minneapolis: Twenty-First Century Books, 2004. Israel is an ancient land—home of the Dead Sea, the Dead Sea Scrolls, and thousands of years of history. This book explores Israel in great depth.

Jenkins, Mark, ed. *Worlds to Explore: Classic Tales of Travel and Adventure from National Geographic.* Washington, DC: National Geographic, 2006. These thrilling, firsthand accounts of explorers and adventurers are gathered from the archives of *National Geographic* magazine.

Johnson, Rebecca. *A Walk in the Rain Forest.* Minneapolis: Lerner Publications Company, 2001. Rain forests are home to countless trees, animals, plants, and insects. Each and every living thing is dependent on all the others. This book examines these fascinating, rainy worlds.

Johnston, Alexa. *Reaching the Summit: Sir Edmund Hillary's Life of Adventure.* New York: Dorling Kindersley, 2005. Follow the story of Edmund Hillary, from his boyhood in New Zealand to his ascent of Mount Everest to the building of a hospital and school for Sherpas. The book includes Hillary family photographs.

McCarty, Nick. *Marco Polo: The Boy Who Traveled the Medieval World.* Washington, DC: National Geographic, 2006. Imagine getting the chance to travel thousands of miles into unexplored territory. In the 1200s, teenage Marco Polo did that and much more.

Winner, Cherie. *Camels.* Minneapolis: Lerner Publications Company, 2008. The Gobi Desert in Mongolia and China is one of two remaining homes for wild Bactrian camels. In this book, Winner offers loads of information about camels and their habitats.

Woods, Michael, and Mary B. Woods. *Disasters Up Close: Volcanoes.* Minneapolis: Lerner Publications Company, 2007. The Woodses explain how volcanoes such as Mount Fuji have altered the face of Earth. They examine how and where volcanoes form and how these fire mountains cause great disasters.

Zuehlke, Jeffrey. *Indonesia in Pictures.* Minneapolis: Twenty-First Century Books, 2006. From rain forests to orangutans, Indonesia is a fascinating place. This book takes an in-depth look at this island nation.

Websites

Cappadocia Guide Online

http://www.cappadociaguideonline.com

Find out all about the incredible stone structures in Cappadocia, formed from volcanic rock. This site includes lots of information about the area's rock-cut churches, underground cities, and other structures.

Everest

http://www.pbs.org/wgbh/nova/everest

At this site, a companion to the PBS *NOVA* television program, you'll learn about the adventurers who try to climb Mount Everest—and both their failures and accomplishments.

Explore Japan: Kids Web Japan

http://web-jpn.org/kidsweb/explore/index.html

This website provides lots of information on Japan, including its culture, climate, and mountains such as Mount Fuji.

Saving Wildlife: Tropical Rainforest Heritage of Sumatra

http://www.wcs.org/international/Asia/Indonesia/trhs

People worldwide are trying to save the Sumatra rain forest. This site offers information on rain forest animals and efforts to protect their habitat.

INDEX

About the Authors

Michael Woods is a science and medical journalist in Washington, D.C. He has won many national writing awards. Mary B. Woods is a school librarian. Their past books include the eight-volume Ancient Technology series, the fifteen-volume Disasters Up Close series, and the seven-volume Ancient Wonders of the World books. The Woodses have four children. When not writing, reading, or enjoying their grandchildren, the Woodses travel to gather material for future books.

Photo Acknowledgments

The images in this book are used with the permission of: © Thomas Kitchin & Victoria Hurst/leesonphoto/drr.net, p. 5; © iStockphoto.com/Guenter Guni, pp. 6, 73 (bottom right); © age fotostock/SuperStock, pp. 8, 23 (top), 38, 39 (top), 46, 54, 57 (bottom), 60 (left), 61, 62 (top); © Galen Rowell/CORBIS, p. 9 (inset); © iStockphoto.com/Stuart Murchinson, p. 9 (main); © Gordon Wiltsie/National Geographic/Getty Images, p. 10 (top); © Hulton Archive/Getty Images, p. 10 (bottom); © Space Frontiers/Hulton Archive/Getty Images, p. 11; © Paula Bronstein/Getty Images, p. 12; © Andy Politz/Mallory & Irvine/Getty Images, p. 13 (top); © Keystone/Hulton Archive/Getty Images, p. 13 (bottom); © Mary Evans Picture Library/Alamy, p. 14; © Devendra M Singh/AFP/Getty Images, p. 15; © Gavriel Jecan/Danita Delimont Agency/drr.net, p. 16; © TNT MAGAZINE/Alamy, p. 18; © Viktor Glupov/Dreamstime.com, p. 19; © Bert Crawshaw/Art Directors & TRIP, p. 20; © Ted Wood/Aurora/Getty Images, p. 21; © Dean Conger/National Geographic/Getty Images, p. 22; © SuperStock, Inc./SuperStock, pp. 23 (bottom), 34; © Liu Jin/AFP/Getty Images, p. 24 (top); © Gina Corrigan/Robert Harding World Imagery/Getty Images, p. 24 (bottom); © Louie Psihoyos/Science Faction/Getty Images, p. 25; © Steve Vidler/SuperStock, p. 26; © Karen Kasmauski/National Geographic/Getty Images, pp. 28 (top), 32, 35 (inset); © Réunion des Musées Nationaux/Art Resource, NY, p. 28 (bottom); © Tibor Bognar/Art Directors & TRIP, p. 29; © iStockphoto.com/Mikhail Kusayev, p. 30 (top); © Damon Coulter/Alamy, p. 30 (bottom); © Simon Heaton/SuperStock, p. 31 (inset); © Akira Isonishi/Sebun Photo/Getty Images, p. 31 (main); © Kazuhiro Nogi/AFP/Getty Images, p. 33; AP Photo/Shizuo Kambayashi, p. 35 (main); © tbkmedia.de/Alamy, p. 36; © Wolfgang Kaehler/drr.net, pp. 39 (bottom), 73 (bottom center); © Travel Ink/Gallo Images/Getty Images, p. 40 (main); © Chris Gray/Art Directors & TRIP, p. 40 (inset); © Paul Debois/Gap Photos/Visuals Unlimited, p. 41 (left); © Tom and Pat Leeson/drr.net, p. 41 (right); © iStockphoto.com/Alina Solovyova-Vincent, p. 42 (top); © Peter Horree/Alamy, p. 42 (bottom); © Ian Waldie/Getty Images, p. 43 (top); © Ahmad Zamroni/AFP/Getty Images, pp. 43 (bottom), 44 (bottom); © Andrew Holt/Photographer's Choice RF/Getty Images, p. 44 (top); AP Photo/Bullit Marquez, FILE, p. 45; © Uriel Sinai/Getty Images, p. 48; © Hemis.fr/SuperStock, p. 49 (both); © Mark Rogers/Art Directors & TRIP, p. 50; © Jon Arnold Images/SuperStock, p. 51; © Dagmar Sizer/Art Directors & TRIP, p. 52 (top); AP Photo/CP, Paul Chiasson, p. 52 (bottom); AP Photo/Nader Daoud, p. 53; © iStockphoto.com/Tomas Bercic, p. 56 (main); © Michele Burgess/SuperStock, p. 56 (inset); © Cuneyt Oguztuzun/Images & Stories/drr.net, p. 57 (top); © David Sutherland/drr.net, p. 58 (top); © Erich Lessing/Art Resource, NY, p. 58 (bottom); © Mauritius/SuperStock, pp. 59, 60 (bottom right); © Frits Meyst/Adventure4ever.com/drr.net, p. 60 (top right); © Shai Eynav/SuperStock, p. 62 (bottom); © Yoray Liberman/Getty Images, p. 63; © LOOK Die Bildagentur der Fotografen GmbH/Alamy, pp. 64, 69 (left); © Tim Laman/National Geographic/Getty Images, pp. 66, 73 (top center); © Michele Falzone/Alamy, p. 67; © Henry Westheim Photography/Alamy, pp. 68, 69 (right); © Tom Till/drr.net, p. 70 (main); © vario images GmbH & Co.KG/Alamy, p. 70 (inset); © Ewan Chesser/Dreamstime.com, p. 71; © iStockphoto.com/Jillian Pond, p. 73 (top left); © Fotolia.com - Andy Melia, p. 73 (top right); © Richard Ashworth/Robert Harding World Imagery/Getty Images, p. 73 (bottom left); © Koji Nakano/Sebun Photo/Getty Images, p. 73 (center right). Illustrations by © Laura Westlund/Independent Picture Service.

Front Cover: © iStockphoto.com/Jillian Pond (top left); © John Lander/drr.net (top center); © iStockphoto.com/Guenter Guni (top right); © Koji Nakano/Sebun Photo/Getty Images (center); © Richard Ashworth/Robert Harding World Imagery/Getty Images (bottom left); © Wolfgang Kaehler/drr.net (bottom center); © Fotolia.com-Andy Melia (bottom right).